GRAPHIC LIBRARY

GREAT ESCAPES OF WORLD WAR II

# TUNNELLING TO FREEDOM

## THE GREAT ESCAPE FROM STALAG LUFT III

by Nel Yomtov

raintree

a Capstone company — publishers for children

Raintree is an imprint of Capstone Global Library Limited, a company incorporated in England and Wales having its registered office at 264 Banbury Road, Oxford, OX2 7DY – Registered company number: 6695582

www.raintree.co.uk
myorders@raintree.co.uk

Editor: Christopher Harbo
Art Director: Nathan Gassman
Designer: Ted Williams
Media Researcher: Wanda Winch
Production Specialist: Gene Bentdahl
Illustrator: Alessandro Valdrighi

ISBN 978 1 4747 3216 1
21 20 19 18 17
10 9 8 7 6 5 4 3 2 1

British Library Cataloguing in Publication Data
A full catalogue record for this book is available from the British Library.

Design Elements: Shutterstock: aodaodaodaod,
paper texture, esfera, map design,
Natalya Kalyatina, barbed wire design

All of the internet addresses (URLs) given in this book were valid at the time of going to press. However, due to the dynamic nature of the internet, some addresses may have changed, or sites may have changed or ceased to exist since publication. While the author and publisher regret any inconvenience this may cause readers, no responsibility for any such changes can be accepted by either the author or the publisher.

Printed and bound in China.

# CONTENTS

PRISONERS
OF THE NAZIS............4

BREAK OUT! ...........6

HEROES ALL............28

GLOSSARY.................... 30

COMPREHENSION QUESTIONS ........31

READ MORE .................... 31

WEBSITES .................... 32

INDEX .................... 32

# PRISONERS OF THE NAZIS

During World War II (1939–1945), Allied forces flew thousands of bombing missions over Germany and Nazi-occupied territory in Europe. The goal of the missions was to knock out railways, harbours, factories and oil resources. Almost any enemy activity that helped the German war effort was a target for the Allied bombers.

Allied airmen, however, faced stiff resistance from the Germans. Speedy, well-armed German fighter planes, as well as guns positioned on the ground, shot down many Allied aircraft. Those Allied pilots lucky enough to survive being blasted out of the sky and crashing to the ground were captured by German soldiers as prisoners of war.

The captured Allied airmen were sent to prison camps. Prison life was grim, and every prisoner, or *kriegie*, knew he faced possible death. One of the most famous camps was known as Stalag Luft III. A "Stalag Luft" was a prisoner-of-war camp specially built for downed enemy airmen.

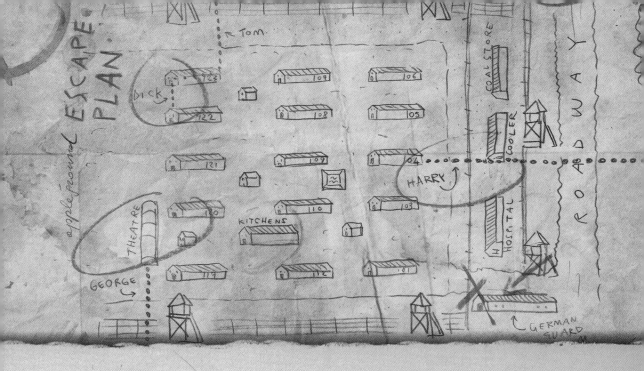

Stalag Luft III was run by the German Air Force. Opened in May 1942, the camp was built to hold Allied officers. It was located near the town of Sagan, about 160 kilometres (100 miles) southeast of Berlin.

Most notably, Stalag Luft III was very secure. The Nazis even claimed the camp was "escape-proof". Tunnelling out of Stalag Luft III was difficult because the soil was sandy. In addition, the Nazis had placed sound detectors in the ground to learn of any tunnelling activities. German guards armed with machine guns kept watch on the prisoners from tall towers overlooking the camp.

Although escape seemed impossible, dozens of tunnel attempts were made at Stalag Luft III by the spring of 1943. Every attempt failed. Still, every prisoner was committed to escaping. As the months wore on, the prisoners' plans of escape became ever more bold and courageous. The time was ripe for a plan to finally succeed.

# BREAK OUT!

My idea is to dig three tunnels at the same time and get about 500 men on the job.

The Germans might find a couple, but we ought to make it with at least one.

Here's my plan . . .

Squadron Leader Roger Bushell of the British Royal Air Force proposed his idea to fellow prisoners.

Each tunnel will be 9 metres deep and have a railway trolley. We'll call the tunnels Tom, Dick and Harry.

Tom and Dick will run out of the camp to the west. Harry will go north.

What do you think?

Sounds risky, but we're in.

The men put the dirt from the tunnels into cloth bags, which they wore inside their trouser legs. When the men pulled a string, the bag opened and the dirt fell out onto the ground.

"Factories" were set up to produce the material needed once the men escaped.

A forgery department created new identities for each escapee. Letters and passes were forged to allow the men to travel through Nazi territories.

The tailoring department was run by Tommy Guest and Ivo Tonder. Most of the tailors were Czech and Polish Air Force officers.

Nice work on that suit, Ivo.

Thanks, Tommy. That German uniform will pass for the real thing too.

Al Hake, an Australian pilot, was put in charge of the compass factory.

*Each man will need a compass to travel the countryside and reach his specific destination.*

Johnny Bull and Johnny Marshall were the first to enter Harry. Their job was to open the escape hatch at the end of the tunnel.

Hurry up, boys. I've got 200 men itching to get out of here.

Good thing we tapped into the Germans' electrical system.

The men might panic if they had to be down here in total darkness.

Minutes later, Marshall joined Bull at the escape hatch. Behind them, many escapees were already in the tunnel.

I can see the stars, Marshall! What a glorious sight!

But wait. Oh, no –!

THE TUNNEL IS TOO SHORT!

Whew! Good thing I made it onto this train. The station will be crawling with German soldiers in no time.

If I'm lucky, the police won't be able to walk through these crowded cars to check my papers.

By 5.00 in the morning, van der Stok was in Breslau, Germany.

I'd like tickets to Alkmaar in the Netherlands. Here are my travel papers.

Everything seems to be in order. Here are your tickets. Have a pleasant trip, Herr Beeldman.

Thank you.

The journey to the Netherlands required three train changes.

At 10.00 in the morning, van der Stok arrived in Dresden, Germany. He decided to enjoy the city before his next train departed.

*Such a magnificent place! Its beauty is astounding. How has it managed to escape the horrors of this terrible war?*

Unfortunately, Dresden would not escape the horrors of World War II much longer. Less than one year later, Allied bombers reduced Dresden to a pile of rubble.

Van der Stok then boarded a train to Hanover that carried him on to Oldenzaal, on the Germany-Netherlands border. When the train arrived, everyone was ordered off to have their papers inspected.

*I knew crossing the border would be the most dangerous part of my escape.*

*By now, my picture has been sent to every Nazi post in the country.*

Van der Stok remained in the Netherlands for six weeks. Some friends helped smuggle him into Belgium on a small boat.

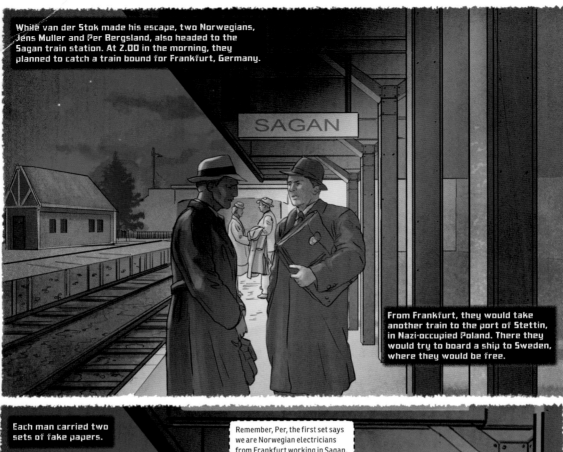

While van der Stok made his escape, two Norwegians, Jens Muller and Per Bergsland, also headed to the Sagan train station. At 2.00 in the morning, they planned to catch a train bound for Frankfurt, Germany.

SAGAN

From Frankfurt, they would take another train to the port of Stettin, in Nazi-occupied Poland. There they would try to board a ship to Sweden, where they would be free.

Each man carried two sets of fake papers.

Remember, Per, the first set says we are Norwegian electricians from Frankfurt working in Sagan.

The second is for our journey from Frankfurt to Stettin. Those papers order us as the same electricians to change our place of work from Frankfurt to Stettin.

Showing the wrong papers could mean certain death.

23

25

# HEROES ALL

Though only three of the 76 escapees reached freedom, the breakout from Stalag Luft III achieved its main goal. Thousands, if not millions, of German civilians, police and military personnel were tied up hunting for the escapees for many weeks. Their efforts prevented them from doing their more important work to help the Nazi war effort.

Back in England, Bob van der Stok rejoined the British Royal Air Force. He flew Spitfire fighters in Operation Overlord, the code name for D-Day, or the invasion of Western Europe, in June 1944. The following year he was placed in command of a Dutch squadron in the Netherlands. There he learned that his two brothers had been killed in concentration camps and the Nazis had blinded his father.

Bob van der Stok

Ray Langlois

Johnny Bull

Roger Bushell

Jens Muller and
Per Bergsland

Len Trent

Al Hake

After the war, van der Stok moved to the United States and worked for the National Aeronautics and Space Administration (NASA) and the US Coast Guard. He died in 1993 at age 78.

Per Bergsland and Jens Muller went to Canada for the rest of the war. After the conflict, both men worked for Norwegian airline companies. Bergsland died in 1992 at age 74. Muller died in 1999 at age 82.

Today the escape from Stalag Luft III is known as The Great Escape. Everyone involved — the planners, the diggers, the watchmen, the forgers, the tailors and many more — contributed to this legendary flight to

# GLOSSARY

**airman** person in the air force

**air raid** attack in which bombs are dropped from aircraft onto ground targets

**Allied forces** countries united against Germany during World War II, including Great Britain, France, the United States, Canada and others

**barracks** building where soldiers are housed

**concentration camp** prison camp where thousands of inmates are held under harsh conditions

**destination** place to which one is travelling

**escapee** person who has escaped

**forgery** illegal copy of something, such as a document

**Nazi** member of the National Socialist Party led by Adolf Hitler that controlled Germany before and during World War II

**refugee** person forced to leave his or her home because of natural disaster or war

**Resistance** secret group of fighters that worked against the Nazis in occupied countries of Europe during World War II

**smuggle** bring something or someone into or out of a country illegally

# COMPREHENSION QUESTIONS

**1.** Make a list of the skills you think the prisoners required to make the escape. As you do, consider all stages of the breakout, including planning, digging, forging and other phases of work.

**2.** This book begins with narrative text, changes to comic book storytelling and ends with narrative text. Why did the author set up the book this way? How does this structure help you better understand the story?

**3.** Assume the identity of a prisoner in a Stalag Luft during World War II. Write a diary entry telling your experiences from your point of view. Describe your job as an Allied airman, your capture by the Germans, life in the camp, your decision to participate in the breakout or not and other details.

# READ MORE

*Great Escapes* (War Stories), Charlotte Guillain (Heinemann Library, 2012)

*Secrets of World War II* (Top Secret Files), Sean McCollum (Raintree, 2017)

*Spies and Code Breakers* (Heroes of World War II), Claire Throp (Heinemann-Raintree, 2016)

*World War II Visual Encyclopedia* (DK History 10), DK (DK Children, 2015)

# WEBSITES

**www.bbc.co.uk/schools/primaryhistory/world_war2/world_at_war/**
Learn all about the world at war at this BBC website.

**www.ducksters.com/history/world_war_ii/**
Check out this website to learn more about World War II, including spies and secret agents working during the war.

**http://therealgreatescape.com/stalag-luft-iii/**
Learn more about the Great Escape at this website dedicated to the heroism of the escapees from Stalag Luft III.

# INDEX

Allied forces  4

Bergsland, Per  10, 22–25, 27, 29
Bull, Johnny  11, 12, 29
Bushell, Roger  6, 9, 12, 13, 15, 23

escape attempt
    main escape  11–15
    Muller and Bergsland escape  22–27
    van der Stok escape  16–21

forged documents  8, 12, 22

Guest, Tommy  8

Hake, Al  8

Langlois, Ray  14

Marshall, Johnny  11, 12
Muller, Jens  10  22–25, 27, 29

Nazis  4, 5, 8, 15, 19, 20, 21

prisoners of war  4
prison guards  5, 9, 15, 25

Shand, Mick  15
Stalag Luft III  4, 5, 21, 27, 28
    history of  5
    location of  5

Tonder, Ivo  8
Trent, Len  14
tunnels
    construction of  6, 7
    names of  6, 7, 9, 11
    problems with  5

van der Stok, Bob  10, 16–21, 22, 28, 29

## TITLES IN THIS SET

**BEHIND ENEMY LINES:**
The Escape of Robert Grimes with the Comet Line

**DEATH CAMP UPRISING:**
The Escape from Sobibor Concentration Camp

**OUTRUNNING THE NAZIS:**
The Brave Escape of Resistance Fighter Sven Somme

**TUNNELLING TO FREEDOM:**
The Great Escape from Stalag Luft III